A SONG FOR LOST SOULS VOL. I

a song for lost souls
vol. i

TYLER LOISELLE

Tyler Loiselle

Collapse the words
off of your lips
and into this sea
of unfinished needs

Soul shattered pleas
colored to her liking.
And no sense of where
this boat of lies leads.

She'll wrap you up together
Underneath the sweater
The violet tether,
a noose attached to your heart.

Patience tested.
Loneliness compromised.
An argument with
my mind's eye.

Could stability
change this?
Or collapse the cause?
Encouraging.
Understanding.

All of this without pause.

And a justification
of feud.

Could your inner beauty
outshine this light
reflected view.

A symphony of high regard
Assimilating these two hearts
As one chose to flee. Depart.

The journey to find one's soul
The journey to make one whole

Understand,
it's not for you to decide
on another's freedom.
Another's pride.

Here's an apology:

For those that chose to think
that it has taken a while
we merely sought our place
and away from all the noise

It is ideal. Worthwhile.

You are painting in my mind
with colors I've never seen.

With my meaning defined
caught my soul in between

a wonderful muse aligned
and the end of a smoke screen.

She keeps her sunshine
in the back pocket
of her favorite jeans;
hidden in darkness.

She will only share it with the world
when the world
chooses darkness.

If only she knew what the world could have used
before the world
needed her to

Unnecessary reflections
A cold winter morning
Shudder to think
A lover in mourning

Infatuation, protection
A touch so necessary
Quarrels over perfection
A soft breath, extraordinary

Admire the painted colors
Amongst the sky, you look
First Grieve, then explore
Make Due with the path you took.

The light in your heart is out.
No one's home.
White flag waves from the depths.
Past unfolds.

She will find your S.O.S.
Send the signal.
As if words are enough.
You're unspoken for.

Reminder. Remind her.
Break an oath.
Reminder. Remind her.
Turn the light on.

broken
motion,

what's the commotion

we are all puzzles
impossible to solve

until you understand

every maze within you
leads back to the heart.

Rekindle. Reignite.
the dance in moonlight
heart beats. time freeze.
the music is the frigid breeze

Reconcile. Invite.
a soft voice, "love life"
mostly shivers. nervous stares.
the music lessens those fears

Cordial. Caress.
the stars bare your skin. undressed.
thunder now. lightning follows.
can you erase all her sorrows?

She hides in her own shadow
petrified of being embraced.
Dust in her eyes; or just a tear?

Unknown, his journey ahead
Unknown, the embrace she dreads
Unknown, the eventual events

The risks they deservedly take
the heart to heartbreak,
healing each other.

Soul's embrace.

Sink, sink into the midst
what's beneath is waiting
for it is a closing door
of impatient jest.

Don't you see?

Sink, sink into the midst
what was beneath, waits
no longer. For now
must rest.

trust unearned in an undeserving world
a floating promise, never spoken, cold.
troubling, the thought of this silence.

comfortable being uncomfortable
in a complete aberration

pardon me, pardon me.
courage is not my strong suit.

I've torn this map to shreds,
too many times to count.
It's as if it disregards
where I want to go.

Though,

I suppose the map is not at fault.
After all there is no path chosen
there is no path to roam.

I'm going to sleep
with you in my heart
and your courage in my thoughts

understand what I knew was only enough

our time was brief,
our connection was real.
our thoughts were perceived
under premises revealed

I'll love you for the love you showed
and the heart you gave
for a life unknown

Follow me into the hollow
where every word is heard,
every glance noticed.

Follow me into the depths
no feelings are discarded
freedom to discuss what you think.

Follow me into tomorrow
but take it slow tonight
for when the sun rises you will leave.

hear her roar.
feel her strength.

it will echo.
it will vibrate.

through you.
through her.

you can go there
you have the key
there is no spare

unlock and enter
what is inside, stays
stays forever

when you depart
the secrets remain
moreover, a counterpart

quake. quake.
stumble through the buzzards.
cowards arose.

make due
awake the darkness
and madness exposed.

Maybe now you will perceive
what I have always seen

you can carry burdens
buried in your chest

heart wil spill
mind will rest

more tired than not
drifting between the clouds
though shifts

transparency aligns
with who you really are
and it becomes perfectly clear

perpetual sense means
tomorrow is just a glimmer
today is just a thought

Unmistakable calculations
if you read between the lines
immersion, insensitive, cowardice, kind

motions with emotion
and rhythm defined.
finding a purpose without having to rewind

You seek what hasn't been sought.

If adversity was a drug
you would overdose in a drought.

Your hollowness can be filled
with a willing thought.

In defense of all you are
no monster, just subside.

keep dancing in my head.
your movements invoke feelings
indescribable

on your toes, clarity
on your heels, angst
on your side, always

keep dancing through the dawn
for when I wake
you dance no more

Burnt out.
Solstice comes.
Drifting on & on

If you're waiting
praying for a return
on all you've given,
you really don't
understand giving.

Nurture these words
Give them life
make it so they thrive.

The only way
to let them breathe
Is to become the very words

you speak

There is a light in this room
it needn't be on

There is a flourish of color
it needn't be seen

There is a coast engulfed
it needn't be approached

There is courage inside of you
approach it; see it; turn it on

Gone despair
Gone idea
replace your sorrow
replace your fear

mind empty
mindful
courage still
riches null

dethrone a beggar
neglected affair
desperation gone
path now clear

if you dwell on forever
wear your pride on your sleeve.

with a sober mind,
but a drunk heart
everything you ever knew
everything you ever thought

decide if together is forever
or forever you are torn apart

If you find my soul on fire
don't you dare put it out

let it burn
let it smolder

the path you have lead me down
is thinner, longer, colder.

the burns are scars I favor
because you started the fire

shine through and dance
like a ray of sun through the glass
leave me stranded
as neither a sin, shows much class

who is broken
who has broken a single shred of silence.
words unspoken
are not often shared in kind.

no loss
but one's own courage
oh well
guess I'll lose my mind

and
sometimes
the wind blows
just to remind you

it's there

condemn her
to the depths
of your heart

just
blasé
to escape

my greatest gift
is my greatest curse.

the door to my heart
is always unlocked

oh, the depths
I would have gone

oh, the stories
I would have climbed

oh, the miles
I would have flown

if I knew I had your heart

ask until you feel truth
ask until you know truth
ask

for

you may not know the damage
you have done to someone else
until it's too late

must you turn your cold shoulder
must you give me your deaf ear
with every truth you don't want to hear?

more conviction than a failed thief
more silence than an empty glass
with every lie you love to tell

he is not a mourning person
a morning person

still, he found a good morning
to have a good mourning

I don't know where I am
I don't know where I'll be
I'm starting to misunderstand
all I seem to see

And heart have broken
before they have even fallen
And the only hearts to heal
are the ones we have forgotten

pressure, release the valve
filter, your heart and soul

study, perceive the patterns
moreover, understand the disaster

puncture, wounds will heal
defy, followers seldom get what they want

now we say
being genuine
is being fake

now we say
quality of life
gets in the way

now we say
courage of a person
must be kept at bay

now we say
we
as if it includes me

hell is but a word until you face it
entirely frightening, until you make it
lose yourself in it's vastness, infinite space
posture, posture, carry your posture

in truth, our truths are written
amongst what is left and what is right
or perhaps, it is perceived as
what is wrong and what is spite.

or maybe our tongues have decided
the truth is better left spoken
our conscience decided our fingers
must be best kept dismantled, broken

calm now, come now
lying is on the prowl

this is a reminder
as warm & kind as I am
he can easily be
just as cold
just as heartless
tread carefully
the line
is fine

i am not yours
you are not meant for me
don’t let that stop
our shadows from dancing

and here you are again
asleep at my doorstep
your attempt to find
what you missed

what you missed
in mind & eyes
are those moments
those moments
will never be here again

our time was short
our love was messy

sleep was so often
a secondary desire

and now here I am
left with empty palms

and all you left for me
is my shortness of breath

I never found brevity warm
until your silence melted me
from the inside, out

perhaps you can
stop this melting
with your frozen touch

I'll wrap my arms around fear
because it is so cold
and my pride is so strong
my eyes are so blind
my ears so deaf

I'll believe the fear could warm
rather than believe
it is even possible
for me to turn cold

i haven’t heard from you
but, perhaps it is
not you we blame

apologies
I forgot to suggest

don’t lose touch
because it is the only sense
i have left

I am a wandering heart.

one that always seeks
a sensitive soul

I am a wandering smile

one that always follows
an immeasurable path

I am a wandering truth.

one that always reflects
on the false past

Saw each other through
both beginnings & ends;
dramatic tension causes
the pages to turn

Our separation of love and hate
is no longer the plot
the culmination of both
will be the conclusion

Don't blink, staring down
the eye of the Storm
she is the Lioness
you cannot tame

Who would want to temper
the overflow of chaos?
she is the Phoenix
who will not land

No one should contain
What you were meant to be

I hope you follow
if your chaos leaves

unrest, partly to blame
indifference gets what's left
and this cloud follows to no avail
and this crowd follows to find hate

the body connects to interpret feelings
an empty heart won't avert disaster
hopefully, the hope is left in the chamber
and cloak itself as no danger

pace yourself,
because your guess is as good as mine
erase your mind,
your rapture can be impossible to find
beneath your passion
you will find meaning, purpose
pace yourself
because the window closes in due time

with every empty bottle
the greater heft on me

silence so prominent
I become more deft at ambivalence

coarse in tone
a rhythmic shattering on the floor

still won't lighten the load

the shadows play games
merely for their own amusement
for they don't age
don't feel heartbreak

they can disappear
on a cold, bitter night
but know the warmth of summer
or dance by the wicker fire

they know not why they exist
but only as long as they do
for once it all ends, the heart
they attach themselves, is split in two

what a courageous venture
this porous vessel has had
soaked in oil, not yet aflame
besides, ghouls stay cold and wet

I suppose praise will do it no good
I suppose the journey found it's end
and now this particular match won't light
and now the end begins with a friend

groves of winter's past
gardens of a spring's future
the same sun illuminates

my thoughts startled
when shared aloud
in the garden ready to bloom

bloom she must
for she is the garden
and I the sunset

the tide turning
the clock ticking

I envy your courage

a loud breath
a torrid storm

I admire the pain you take

the silent cries
with a timid guise

I feel the warmth you try to share

It only rains on Sunday
The only day she cries
Believe what you may
Just don't believe her lies

To believe in what she sees
Through the eyes of a sinner
It's not an illness or disease
Just feelings that hinder

She belongs in the time of Charlie
Where her cries would be silent

We don't care, Hardly
We don't care, Hardly

I'd like to pose a question
Is the timing appropriate?
Or does this feeling change?

Are we all stuck?
Or can we change and move within?
I think we can breathe a little deeper
If our souls can allow
Much have I been through

Floating in this winter cloud.

are you happy in this storm
that you created for yourself?
can you see through the raindrops
that fill your eyes?

don't drink the water
the salt will poison
don't think of the past
the remnants will poison

it is only after your faults
that you learn to live with it all
and it's only after we live
that we learn to love at all

shameless
how shameless
is the ghost in your head
and the punishing chill
colder than the cigarette
on your lips

oh, the trouble it is
to be on your tongue
but never by your side.
because the chaos of
a lost Sunday chose
a path of no return

and now a want
has destroyed
what was a
well,
you know...

in two words:
I tried.

trust.
love

as unbreakable
as fragile
as both

unsustainable
this willingness
to cede

it's never worth
the explanation

because the regression
will cause aggression

An old soul came to visit today
with an uncanny resemblance of him
his tired eyes, his soft hands
his skin as rough as autumn leaves

he danced because of the song in his head
he sang because of the sadness he saw
maybe no one saw his true virtue
maybe no one saw his time was gone

until he spoke

"your kind of love
is just not something
I want to be a part of"

Like treasure
but the golden shine
is on the inside

Like fire
attitude burns
igniting passion

Like wind
move
when it's time to go

With every thunderous vibration
I seek an unnamed star
in my endless hope
to know where we are

Waiting for a path to be shown
until lightning strikes
revealing a fire burning
enraptured by a silhouette

Never search twice
where we are is no matter
who you are with
beneath the unnamed star

That is true meaning

punish me under
a convincing sky

day dreams disguised
as focused lies

cut all the lights
this winding road needn't any
for I know where it leads

though I've never driven it
I encounter it in every dream
admiring the path nature leads

bare trees, filled with hope
as each season softens
the cold hearts of those traveling before us

I'm nobody of importance
and that's okay.

I'd rather take my own path
I'd rather love the people that matter

I'm understanding, sure
but I'm not here to oblige

I'll pick and choose
with whom in the world I'll align

waste it on the liars
waste it on the cynics
he told me to waste it on them all

it's never a waste
it's never a drain
it's just a way to keep me sane

the reason you wake with the sun
the reason it moves you
is to brace for the fleeting moments ahead

it's never a waste
it's never a drain
it's just a way to keep me sane

good intentions are meant to be
more than a dream
more of everything

and here we are
paired misfortune
like doves
each with a broken wing

and here we are
palpitations no more
like cacti
surviving on what we store

and here we are
frozen, melting
like icicles
falling in warmth

I knew a liar once
every word a second hand joke
not unlike the soul beneath

“know your craft”
I uttered, a misunderstanding
I’m becoming my own mistake

hiding beneath the false scars
maybe it was a mystery
you always wanted to be

your name a misnomer
always by choice
always by validation

I thought I knew a liar once

pair me with the right one
and unnervingly I'll accept
with unending streams of consciousness
and an apparent air of vigilance

cautious pacing brings treading water
but the boats of hope are prepared
move with the tide, but don't collide
our paths aren't meant to cross

stare me down, without your sympathy
eyeing the storm within me
hush your terrors beneath the calm
patience please, the tide will come

these animalistic tendencies
have gotten the best of you
progress is a beast you cannot tame

no matter, no mind
keep believing you're beyond time
it is entertaining for the jungle

being so far south of the heart
and so far north of the sun
location unknown, forever on

grasp me
like a straw?

stop trying to fit me
into buckets or boxes
like I'm one size fits all

as if you'll get to know me
before I'll know myself

and label me
as one of your own

contemplate what you've known before

I, like you,
am ever-changing

we are so sick of being
punished by the dark
the dark that refuses
to understand the light

we are enabled angels of yesterday
enabled by a storm, unpredictable
because like our hearts
days are partitioned

we are entrusted with trust
abusers of the cause
burdened by praise
from the unrecognized

this false darkness
has merely awakened
the distress call
of the slumbered few

Turn the lights on
it is my time

part of me is ruined
by my own convictions
and the line in the sand I chose to cross

part of me is disheveled
as if taken on by a tornado
traveling through my state of mind

part of me is conflicted
by the startling progressions
I refused to see

part of me is enamored
by the rules you chose to break
they were your own after all

such a kindling, still
you started a fire you can't put out
never putting a caution sign up

nor attempting to drown the flames

amidst all the rain
you had your chance
and with all the cold

all you had to say was you were seeking warmth

plug me in
power me on
select my story

manage a mind
that's your strongest urge
lesson learned

no understanding
no disobeying
no counterbalance

perhaps you'll get a chance to do it again

and the sorrows
the worry
the pain
won't hold off
any tomorrows

but the strengths
the slow breath
the spark ignited
will give you smoke
to float on

forever these drapes
hide nothing but fear
open them wide
believe in hope
and conscience cleared

you'll know I'm always there

through the soft touch of wind
through the lyrics
of a song
through the views of the clouds

you'll know where to find me

not in my old home
not in my old clothes
not in my resting place

you'll always know I'm there
in your heart
you'll know where to find me
within you

soft, so soft
a feature most often
seen as weakness

for him,
strength
for him,
love

why do people
wait for the end
to seek kindness
to seek warmth
to seek a soft heart?

from lust to lust
and liar to liar
no beats ever skipped
no feelings ever kept

why does the heart,
why does the mind,
must they disconnect?

or perhaps the question is
why must they be aligned
for your worlds to intersect

it was inaction that cause failure
and a misconception that I
understood
it was inaction that left you
chasing your tail
now a constant reminder of where
I've been left
I accept the punishment
the blame and whatever else
you've let me with

I never knew you
and that alone
makes me understand
this is all I ever wanted

cut through to my soul
with a hammer and chisel
a symphony of words
or perhaps a palindrome
and you can unlock
it without a key
only you forgot
to read the instructions

the coldest days are the silent ones
the warmest nights are the silent ones
we treat both the same
why do we feel inadequacy regardless?
why does our focus move with both?
why is your life dictated by the silence you receive?

no two silent days are the same

trust when what is said
has meaning
trust when what is said
has care
but what if they have neither
in a departure
an escape
they arrive empty
unkempt, barren

oh well, if only you could
return on receipt

follow me into the hollow
where every word is heard
every glance, noticed.

follow me into the depths
no feelings are discarded
freedom to discuss what you think

follow me into tomorrow
but take it slow tonight
for when the sun rises, you will leave

blatantly clear of my intentions
a sucker for absence
because of the cost of
your presence is inflated

predicting my exit
before the end is near
and I'm just chaos
personified

sorry if you misunderstood
I'm just addicted to new

my words have dried up
like blood clotting a wound

only rather than healing
now an endless affliction

I once tempted
you with my tongue

you've always haunted me
with your absence

destined to dance til death
together but apart

the sails took hold
of the wind.
Panic struck, all but one

He needn't worry.

For it was not the Captain's offense.
Nor was it his men's.

Was the guide
who lead us astray.

'A miscalculation,'
an excuse.
He was shallow,
and wretched.

Captain knew, as it was
his time.

But for the guide,
must find a new life to sink.

seize me
as curiosity finds courage
to expose truths beneath
a sea of burdens

and despite the squalls
the stories to be told
will be of virtue and wealth

or love by definition

and understand
this misunderstanding is
needed

seize me
through the sea of burdens

with a sober mind
and a drunk heart
you dwell on forever
as if the moment won't escape

everything you ever knew
everything you ever thought

decide if it's forever together
or forever torn apart

Time after time
Chance after chance
and every question
is answered with a dance
Because words mean nothing
And neither do these songs
but perhaps what has meaning
hasn't come along

Punish your demons
They're not the real you
They're conspiring
Against your good heart
Challenging your patience
Challenging your courage
Protect your spirit
Fearlessly

I expected you to ground me
Keep my head out of the clouds
Yet the hurricane came
I floated above to see it through
And it was a storm with less chaos
than you

I'd sparkle in the sun
but I'm much too bitter
to squander the thoughts
of that sweet sinner

I'd glance at the moonlight
but it's too close to home
and I'd only do it out of spite

instead

I'd rather shut my eyes
than have the light be shown

find your peace
because the waves
have finally calmed

but if you keep
looking for waves
you're testing waters
in the hope of sinking
your own ship

take a moment
to take a moment

notice the space
change the pace
of the life you're living
because caution does not care
and caring is too cautious

a moment
that is all it took
a moment of space
a moment of caution
and now that moment is gone

www.ingramcontent.com/pod-product-compliance
Lightning Source LLC
Chambersburg PA
CBHW071539100726
47908CB00004B/1437

* 9 7 8 1 7 3 5 9 3 4 1 0 5 *